COUNTER

THE
ANTIOXIDANT
COUNTER

*A Pocket Guide
to the Revolutionary
ORAC Scale for
Choosing Healthy Foods*

Dr. Mariza Snyder & Dr. Lauren Clum

Ulysses Press

Published by Ulysses Press
      P.O. Box 3440
      Berkeley, CA 94703
      www.ulyssespress.com

ISBN: 978-1-56975-866-3
Library of Congress Catalog Number 2010937116

Printed in Canada by Webcom

10 9 8 7 6 5 4 3 2 1

Acquisitions Editor: Kelly Reed
Managing Editor: Claire Chun
Editor: Susan Lang
Proofreader: Lauren Harrison
Production: Judith Metzener
Cover design: Double R Design (front), what!design @ whatweb.com (back)
Interior design and layout: what!design @ whatweb.com
Cover photos: blueberries © haveseen/istockphoto.com, wine © mjp/istockphoto.com, pepper © subjug/istockphoto.com

Distributed by Publishers Group West

NOTE TO READERS
This book has been written and published strictly for informational and educational purposes only. It is not intended to serve as medical advice or to be any form of medical treatment. You should always consult your physician before altering or changing any aspect of your medical treatment and/or undertaking a diet regimen, including the guidelines as described in this book. Do not stop or change any prescription medications without the guidance and advice of your physician. Any use of the information in this book is made on the reader's good judgment after consulting with his or her physician and is the reader's sole responsibility. This book is not intended to diagnose or treat any medical condition and is not a substitute for a physician.

We dedicate this book to our patients
at The Specific Chiropractic Center,
who have been the guiding force
and inspiration for this book and
who have taught us so much.

TABLE OF CONTENTS

Introduction   9

Chapter 1: What Should I Eat?   12

Chapter 2: Antioxidants   25

Chapter 3: The ORAC Scale   50

Chapter 4: Recipes   74

About the Authors   128

INTRODUCTION

As chiropractors, our job is to help our patients navigate the sometimes treacherous, or at the very least confusing, path to health and wellness. During our years of working with patients, we realized several things, two of which stand out. First, it is absolutely amazing how many people are suffering from chronic pain, hypertension, heart disease, cancer, and other chronic, degenerative diseases. Second, most people have very little idea about how much their daily decisions affect their overall health.

One area that individuals do have control over is what goes into their bodies. Unfortunately, so many people are constantly on the go, consuming lots of junk in the form of processed foods and fast foods. This is an age when processed foods are found in great abundance and antioxidant-rich foods have fallen by the wayside. Despite the number of farmer's markets and the amount of fresh produce available, many people just don't know how to choose and cook organic, antioxidant-rich fruits and vegetables. Often they can't name the most common or healthiest foods available at their local stores and don't know what antioxidants are or how they can transform the body.

We realized that often people want to make healthy decisions but simply need some guidance in making that happen. So we began to put together lists of what we call "super foods" (page 42) along with recipes and nutritional guidelines to help our patients transition to healthy eating, not only to aid in the healing process but to ensure continued health and vitality. As we reach out beyond the walls of our practice, our intention remains the same: to keep healthy eating simple by providing clearly defined nutritional information for the average person to use every day.

We hope you will use this book as a guide to healthy eating and living. Our goal is to give you a grasp of the ORAC (Oxygen Radical Absorbance Capacity) scale and a practical understanding of antioxidants and the many benefits of whole foods. A majority of the essential nutrients that everyone needs on a daily basis are found in the foods—specifically fruits, vegetables, and herbs—listed in this book. We have formatted it to be a handy reference that will make it easier for you to choose whole, antioxidant-rich foods when you're at the supermarket and farmer's market. These foods provide a framework for preventing and fighting chronic diseases.

We'll delve into the ORAC scale in detail later in the book. Right now, it's important to know that the ORAC unit, or ORAC value, is a method of measuring the antioxidant capacity of various foods. The scale is primarily used to ascertain which foods have the highest antioxidant values. By referring to this book, you'll be able to quickly identify the healthiest foods— the ones that fight the damaging, disease-causing molecules called free radicals—and learn how to put that antioxidant power to practical use.

CHAPTER 1

What Should I Eat?

One of the most common questions that our patients ask us is, "What should I eat?" That's not surprising given all of the conflicting information about nutrition and diet. One day you hear about how harmful fats are to overall health and how they lead to heart disease and chronic illness, only to learn the very next day that "low-fat" food products are bad because of added preservatives and refined sugars. Nutrition has become a very confusing landscape riddled with contradictions about what is healthy and what is not. It's no wonder everyone is so confused.

Conflicting nutritional advice comes from a variety of sources—doctors and other health practitioners, the media, diet books, government initiatives, and industrialized corporate food companies—all throwing around words like "low-fat," "omega-3s," "antioxidants," "high fiber," and "gluten free," in order to sell products or explain nutrition. What does all of this mean, and how do you separate what is truly healthy to eat from complicated nutritional health claims that may be untrue and unhealthy?

Over the years much research has been done on the topic of healthy foods and nutritionally healthy diets. We, as a society, learned that we did not necessarily know what it means to eat healthy. What we thought was healthy turned out to be saturated with processed, unhealthy junk, and what we thought was unhealthy may turn out to be integral to body function. With all of this clashing information, we, as practitioners, began to understand why our patients were frustrated about gaining weight and becoming unhealthy while following what seemed to be good nutritional advice. We also found that our patients, and people generally, were looking for a magic bullet to avoid obesity, heart disease, and other conditions such as cancer, type 2 diabetes, and chronic fatigue.

While there is no magic bullet, we discovered many useful things about nutrition, diet, and health that we'd like to share. We learned that it wasn't about eating less of one nutrient and more of another. It wasn't about splitting up nutrients to try and get the most out of just one. It is actually far simpler than that. We learned that the easiest way to be healthy is to eat real food. Doesn't get much simpler, does it? We hope that once people understand what is causing them to become overweight and sick, they will be ready to make the necessary changes and move toward whole, natural foods.

Our society is dominated by the Western food diet, or Western food pattern, which consists of lots of processed foods, meats, fats, and sugar. And whether intentionally or not, it also includes preservatives, additives, hormones, and genetically modified ingredients that the human body is unable to metabolize properly, if at all. Researchers now know that people who follow this diet commonly end up with chronic diseases: obesity, heart disease, diabetes, and cancer. Of the top-10 health-related killers in Western populations, 5 are chronic diseases directly related to diet. This way of eating is causing significant problems in the health of many industrialized nations, killing millions each year.

It's no wonder so many of us are concerned about what to eat. Everyone knows someone who has died of a heart attack or cancer. Many people try to blame genetics, but that argument just isn't believable anymore. At this point, industrialized nations need to stop trying to tweak and change processed foods to be healthier and instead focus on doing away with them altogether. All of us need to begin making changes today, in our individual lives. It has become clear that the Western diet is not paving a road to health; it is forging a path to illness.

Industrial food processing has taken our traditional diet of thousands of edible foods to one consisting of a few main ingredients: processed corn, rice, soy, and processed wheat. While these foods are not intrinsically evil, they have become harmful as a result of the immense processing they go through to become "food." These four ingredients have become mainstays of the diet in America and other industrialized countries. Soy and corn make up more than one-third to as much as two-thirds of our daily diet. Our diet has become a glut of corn- and soy-based products. If you were to go into your pantry right now and pick up a box of cereal, you would likely find corn or soy listed at least two or three times in the ingredients. They have become our main sources of nutrition for a number of reasons, starting with the advent of fast foods. Corn and soy can be produced, manufactured, and delivered inexpensively; they are cheap and readily available for busy families; and they can be nutritionally fortified with vitamins and minerals, which were stripped in the manufacturing process. While this sounds reasonable, the reality is that our limited, monocultural food source is killing us every day, without most people even knowing it.

Let's not forget the most processed and refined carbohydrate of them all: sugar. The biggest change in the Western diet over the past several decades has been the increased consumption of sugar. If you were to include sugar with corn- and soy-based products, then carbohydrates make up 50 to 75 percent of the daily American diet. The remainder of the diet consists of processed meats, fats, and some fruits and vegetables. Given the tremendous amount of refined carbohydrates consumed, it's no wonder obesity and chronic diseases are on the rise.

There is very little nutritional sustenance in refined carbohydrates; they lack the fiber and essential vitamins and minerals the human body needs to function. This nutritional void leads us to eat even more, as our bodies crave nutrients. Consuming empty calories has led us down a slippery slope, tricking our metabolisms into needing more empty calories. This widespread consumption of the Western food diet has given way to a whacked-out metabolism unable to handle the mass amounts of consumed sugar—and type 2 diabetes and obesity are direct consequences. Since the younger generations have been consuming this diet since childhood, we find ourselves in a time when children will die of chronic diseases before their parents.

Luckily, there are still places in the world where processed ingredients have not pervaded farms, factories, supermarkets, and homes. Many populations, such as in Chile, Australia, Greenland, and Japan, are still consuming a variety of traditional foods that have been passed down from generation to generation. They show a significantly lower incidence of type 2 diabetes, heart disease, and cancer. An interesting fact to note is the great variety of traditional diets, ranging from diets high in fats to ones high in protein, proving that human beings are very adaptable. This means that there is not one particular diet that is superior to the rest, just that a diet consisting of nutritionally void, processed substances is unhealthy. Over the last several decades, the Western food industry has managed to turn what used to be a traditional whole food diet into a conveniently processed diet that makes people chronically sick. It is quite remarkable that in an era of incredible technology and medical advances, many of them spawned here in the United States, ours is one of the sickest industrialized nations in the world.

So when patients ask the inevitable question, "What should I eat?" we say, "Eat real food." Usually they look at us as if we're crazy or didn't hear them properly. What have they been eating if not real food? Prompted by the look of confusion, we explain what real food is and what it isn't. We tell them that most of what's sold in supermarkets is not real food, that an average of 20,000 new processed food products line the shelves every year, replacing what used to be real food. From applesauce to instant rice, packaged bacon to tofu dogs, fake foods have dominated the supermarket shelves for decades, disguised as real food. We go on to say that real foods are whole foods, foods found in nature, foods that you can imagine in their raw state or find growing in natural soil. These are foods that do not go through a processing plant or have more than three to five ingredients listed on the packaging. Real food doesn't claim to be something it isn't; real food doesn't have to make any claims. When's the last time you saw a "gluten-free" sticker on a tomato? Real food is simply not typically found in packages lining the middle aisles and frozen food sections of the local supermarket.

Identifying processed foods has become tricky because they are everywhere: in supermarkets, convenience stores, restaurants, school cafeterias, and our homes. Not only are they everywhere we turn, but a majority of the food-like products being sold today are cleverly disguised as real food. Many packaged food products are marketed as healthy, cheap, easy to prepare, and authentic—which you might believe until you look at the ingredient list. We have all seen or tried the cereal that claims to lower cholesterol and promote weight loss. Some cereals even set health and weight challenges on the box. However, these food products contain preservatives and imitation ingredients such as high-fructose corn syrup, butylated hydroxytoluene, and modified corn starch. The cereals containing these industrialized ingredients, like so many other products on grocery shelves, are not real food; they are industrialized, processed, food-like products.

Even whole foods have been affected by processing. Take milk, for example. A majority of milk comes from cows raised in industrialized factories and fed genetically modified corn and soy, hormones, and antibiotics. Then the milk is stripped of good nutrients and fortified with others. It's hard to say whether milk is a whole food after all of the processing it undergoes. Today's milk is not the milk our grandparents drank; it differs in fat and nutrient content, and it even has a longer expiration date.

Since many whole foods are processed nowadays, knowing which ones to buy can be difficult if you don't know what to look for. In today's nutritional climate, people searching for healthy foods often tend to look for a particular nutrient— and either less or more of it—to consume for a particular outcome. This way of thinking is not the answer to creating a healthy diet; instead it provides the major food companies a way to market their overly processed products by fortifying "nutrients" into the foods. Nutrients like antioxidants, omega-3s, and fiber are injected into processed foods to entice people into buying them. This doesn't make the product or diet healthier; the Western diet is still disguised as something it isn't. This is all about clever marketing, not healthy eating habits. Even as nutrients are switched to keep pace with the newest nutrition fad, poor health and obesity are on the rise. Children are still gaining weight and developing diabetes before the age of 15. People are still taking medication for hypertension and other chronic illnesses. The frustration is building! Clearly, there has to be a better way of living, a better way of eating.

It's important to learn how to identify real food and to steer away from the Western food model. Basically, as a society, we need to go backward in time, to our roots, and begin focusing on where our food once came from: nature and not a processing plant. We also need to take a step back and redefine our understanding of food and health. Remember, focusing on a particular nutrient for a particular outcome only encourages food companies to keep replacing real food with imitation ingredients through nutrient splitting. It's this way of thinking that got us into trouble. Instead, it's important to make positive, healthy food decisions by considering what we eat, how we eat it, and where it came from.

This new way of looking at food, health, culture, and the environment is going to require some effort, time, and money. Many of us have fallen into the habit of eating Western food products because they're fast, inexpensive, and easy to make. Fast food doesn't just come from fast-food restaurants. Historically, we spent more money and time making real food, and we were healthier for it. Many cultures elsewhere in the world still consume traditional diets. People in other countries buy meats and produce fresh almost every day, spend time at home preparing and cooking meals, and consequently are significantly healthier and live higher-quality lives than we do. We need to reclaim and embrace our traditional ways of eating and return to a time when shopping for, preparing, and enjoying meals were activities closer to the heart of daily life.

As you begin to make changes to your diet, remember that eating healthy is really all about eating fresh whole foods from good land and soil. Regain control of your health by making simple changes. Eating healthy can be simple, as can the ingredients in your meals. Keep in mind that an apple is a whole food; applesauce, apple juice, and apple chips are not. If the ingredient list of a food is long and complicated, trade it for a single ingredient like an apple, or a meal consisting of single ingredients, like a salad made of fresh vegetables. Fresh, local, organic produce is the best available because the soil in which it is grown is rich in vitamins and minerals. If it's difficult to find organic, buy fresh produce and rinse it thoroughly to remove any impurities from the surface. Healthy eating takes just a few simple, consistent steps.

When it comes to making cultural and social changes in our eating habits as a society, all of us can begin by focusing on cooking and eating at home with friends and family. When we eat out, we have no control over portion size, ingredients, or food preparation. We regain that control by preparing meals at home. Cooking requires going to the store to buy nutritious whole foods. Cooking also brings people together, which plays a huge role in eating habits. When we eat by ourselves, we tend to eat less healthy food and more of it. It's important to eat with friends and family, as it teaches us to enjoy the food experience at the dining table, while eating less. It also teaches us to slow down our fast-food ways and enjoy the healthy food on our plates. As a society, we are trained to eat fast and on the go or while watching television. The sooner we can step away from these habits on a daily basis, the better off our hearts, minds, and bodies will be. We are better served by being more conscious of eating, so that we may eat more slowly and actually enjoy our food.

Using this book's guidelines and the ORAC scale are great ways to jump-start healthy eating. They will make food shopping and preparation much easier. The book is designed for you to bring along to the store to help you choose fresh whole foods, especially ones packed with antioxidant properties. The recipes also focus on fresh ingredients and provide delicious ways to introduce more antioxidants and real foods into your diet. We encourage you to find additional recipes, similar to the ones in this book, or to make healthy substitutions for any less-than-healthy recipes you already have. After all, the purpose of eating is to nourish our bodies and well-beings.

CHAPTER 2

Antioxidants

Antioxidants, key players in a healthy body, have been a hot topic in recent years, and—fortunately for our society—they've emerged as one of the biggest nutrition trends. As consumers, we have been told that we need to eat certain foods because they contain more antioxidants, which are important in combating free radicals and decreasing diseases such as cancer, type 2 diabetes, and chronic fatigue syndrome. Consumers have trustfully turned to products like pomegranate juice and blueberries to get their antioxidant fix, without really knowing what antioxidant-rich foods do for the body. Although we, as practitioners, are excited to see more people eating fruits and veggies to get antioxidants, we feel it's just as important for everyone to realize that fruits and veggies serve many purposes in the body, not just to keep free radicals from overwhelming organs and cells. When we make food recommendations to our patients, we include many antioxidant-rich foods, simply because they are the whole foods found in nature, providing the building blocks for healthier, sustainable lives.

We believe that people are more likely to do something when they understand why it's important. Here's a brief background on antioxidants and their job in the body to give you a better understanding of why you should eat antioxidant-rich whole foods every day. As you get into the details, keep the big picture in mind: antioxidants are among the best natural disease fighters, protecting our bodies from everyday stresses that would otherwise wreak havoc on the cellular structures that hold us together.

The primary task of antioxidants is to stop free radicals before they damage the body. Free radicals are primarily a by-product of oxygen. During aerobic metabolism, every cell in the body utilizes oxygen to make energy so that it can do its job. Just as burning wood forms smoke as a by-product, the body creates by-products called free radical oxidants, or free radicals, when cells burn oxygen. These dangerous free radicals cause extra oxygen to damage cells in the body as they react to molecules in and around the cells. A free radical floating around in the body seeks another molecule to make it whole. Unfortunately, when it binds to another molecule, it tears cell walls, rips pieces of DNA, or changes the chemistry of cell structures. When this little bit of damage is magnified by millions per second, the body suddenly has a disaster on its hands. Over time this cellular damage ages the body and facilitates various disease processes. Antioxidants prevent this negative cascade of events, which explains why it's so important that you always have adequate antioxidant levels in your body to protect you.

The formation of free radicals in the body is a normal process; it happens as a result of breathing. However, the following factors contribute to the increased production of free radicals.

+ **STRESS**—Physical, chemical, and emotional stressors are silent intruders that play a huge role in free radical formation and damage. Stress by itself is neither good nor bad; it just is. The variable is how the body responds to stress, and the response is not always positive. The sheer number of stressors present in modern life invite stress-induced illness through chronic damage to organs and cellular structures. Stress from the daily pressures of work, finances, and family forces the body into a sympathetic state, activating a fight or flight response. This defense mechanism causes blood to be shunted toward the extremities and away from the internal organs, burning a lot of energy so that you are physically able to fight or flee. This is meant to be a temporary response because the body is not designed to sustain it for long periods. However, chronic stress keeps the body in this state, and inflammation is created initially to combat the effects.

Inflammation is the body's natural response to an infection or injury, and all inflammatory reactions in the body release free radicals as a by-product. Chronic stress can induce inflammation in our organs, joints, and blood vessels, increasing the release of free radicals, which in turn causes more inflammation. This vicious cycle turns into a crazy spiral and is the culprit in many chronic diseases. The increase in free radical production that comes with stress and inflammation also decreases immune system function throughout the body. That's why you tend to become sicker when your stress levels are steady and high. If your body is under chronic stress (physical, emotional, or chemical), you have chronic inflammation. Hypertension and arthritis are notable examples of inflammation at work.

+ **AUTO EXHAUST AND POLLUTION**—This chemical stress is due to today's industrial lifestyle. Instead of breathing just oxygen, you also breathe carbon monoxide and hydrochloric acid, which create more free radicals in the body. Exhaust fumes irritate the body and contribute to chronic inflammation, which increases cytokine production. An overproduction of cytokines leads to chronic inflammatory conditions such as cancer, asthma, and immune system disorders.

+ **CIGARETTE SMOKE**—Another chemical stress, tobacco smoke impacts both smokers and nonsmokers. Inhaling it affects the body much like breathing polluted air, except that the smoke is concentrated. Cigarette smoke contains more than 3,000 known poisons. The free radicals created by the smoke damage DNA, weaken the immune system by mutating whole blood cells, and increase heart disease by damaging the interior walls of blood vessels and causing blood clots.

+ **RADIATION**—Exposure to x-rays, sunlight, and natural radiation in the environment alters molecules in subtle ways, scattering free radicals in the body and cells. Increased radiation exposure leads to cellular mutations, causing degenerative disorders and cancer.

+ **IMPURE WATER**—Impurities in municipal water supplies and the chemicals used to cover up those pollutants are responsible in part for a buildup of toxins in the body. Most tap water, and some bottled water, contains toxic impurities and up to 500 different disease-causing viruses, bacteria, and parasites. That's why we recommend against drinking large quantities of tap water and instead drinking filtered, purified, or distilled water.

+ **TOXIC METALS**—Many industrial waste products find their way into the soil, water supply, air, and food. Heavy metals are also present in cosmetics, cooking utensils, paints, plastics, solvents, and health care products. These toxic metals attract free radicals and carry them to the brain, liver, and other vital organs. Once the metals enter the body, they remain there and accumulate. Lead and mercury, the best-known toxic metals, cause central nervous system disorders and degeneration of the brain.

+ **PROCESSED FOODS**—Many of the chemical additives found in processed foods create havoc in the body. They often can't be broken down and lead to an increased production of free radicals, contributing to an array of chronic diseases. Much of the produce sold today is saturated with pesticides, herbicides, protective wax, and contaminants to prevent spoilage while the food is transported long distances to supermarkets. Meat and dairy come from cows that have been pumped full of antibiotics and fed diets primarily of processed corn and soy, making them dangerous to consume. Chronic disease is increasing at alarming rates due to the rise of man-made foods.

+ **DRUGS**—Whether they are prescription, non-prescription, or over-the-counter, drugs are toxins. They change the body's ability to metabolize oxygen, and they contribute to serious side effects by altering the molecular structure of proteins and receptor sites on cell membranes. Long-term and repetitive prescription drug use typically result in the deficiency of essential nutrients, including vital antioxidants, by blocking their absorption, deactivating them, and destroying them. Drugs weaken the body, so we highly recommend consuming whole foods and whole food supplements, particularly when taking medications.

Now that we have covered the biggest factors that increase free radical damage in the body, let's talk about how to combat those processes with antioxidants from whole foods and natural supplements.

As explained earlier, antioxidants are molecules that battle damaging oxidants (free radicals). When the body has enough antioxidants to fight damage, it stays healthier and doesn't age as quickly. But an insufficient amount of antioxidants means that free radicals run rampant, often leading to a multitude of chronic degenerative diseases and aging the body in the process.

Antioxidants protect the body with four levels of defense:

[1] Antioxidants keep free radicals from forming in the first place. They also prevent

heavy metals from sparking oxidation.
Prevention is vital, since oxidation causes the
body to break down and become weak.

[2] Antioxidants intercept oxidizing radicals
that have already formed and stop them
from multiplying. Unless the body has ample
defenses, oxidizing chain reactions will make
it vulnerable to further damage.

[3] The antioxidant defense system gets to
work on damage already caused by oxidation.
The body has an amazing ability to heal,
and with this defense system it can clean up
messes already in progress. Antioxidants go
through and wipe out oxidants.

[4] Antioxidants remove molecules that are
severely damaged and beyond repair. During
this process, antioxidants clean up the debris
and toxins generated by free radical damage.

THE WORLD OF ANTIOXIDANTS

Antioxidants come in many forms including amino
acids, bioflavonoids, enzymes, carotenoids, vitamins,

and minerals. Since antioxidants work in synergy, some of the categories overlap. Let's touch on the major players in the antioxidant world, many of which are found in the foods we eat—or should be eating—every day.

Amino acids

Playing a critical role in biochemical processes involving antioxidants, hormones, and enzymes, amino acids are essential to our overall health by maintaining cellular structures. The three most important antioxidant amino acids are alpha-lipoic acid, cysteine, and glutathione; they fight numerous cancers as well as heart disease and diabetes. Alpha-lipoic acid is the universal antioxidant, ideal in promoting anti-aging. It interacts with vitamins E and C, increasing their effect on the body. A healthy body makes alpha-lipoic acid on its own, but it can be taken as a supplement when needed. Cysteine is known as a free radical scavenger essential in the formation of glutathione, a powerful antioxidant derived from three amino acids. Glutathione's job is to neutralize oxidants in the body by bonding to a toxin and breaking it down into removable parts.

(Glutathione has gained fame in recent years for good reason, affording it its very own section on page 48.)

Bioflavonoids

These naturally occurring compounds found in plants act primarily as plant pigments and antioxidants. They perform a host of biological activities and are especially known for their amazing antioxidant properties. Bioflavonoids are found in berries, grapes, oranges, lemons, bell peppers, turmeric, cinnamon, cumin, and green tea—and many other fruits, vegetables, and spices. The more colorful fruits and vegetables you eat, the more protection you get from these powerful flavonoids and polyphenols.

Carotenoids

Considered phytonutrients, carotenoids are the elements that give fruits and veggies their odor and vibrant color. The best-known and best-understood carotenoids are beta-carotene, lycopene, lutein, and alpha-carotene. However, there are more than five hundred carotenoids known to date. Carotenoid compounds are responsible for the red, orange, and yellow colors of fruits and veggies, and are also found in leafy dark green veggies. Many carotenoids are classified as provitamins, meaning they're precursors to the formation of vitamin A. As such, they assist in preventing vitamin A deficiency and protect against aging, cancer, and heart disease, in addition to boosting immune function and cellular communication. Carrots, squash, sweet potatoes, kale, spinach, tomatoes, grapefruit, bell peppers, and other vibrant vegetables all contain carotenoids.

Vitamins

Needed in small amounts, vitamins are micronutrients that serve diverse biochemical functions. They are essential regulators for cellular function. Vitamins A, C, and E—the ACE vitamins—are antioxidant powerhouses that prevent as well as clean up free radical damage.

Vitamin A is a fat-soluble vitamin that maintains healthy soft tissue, bones, and mucous membranes, and produces pigment in the retina of the eye. The active form of vitamin A is retinol, which promotes good vision. Vitamin A also promotes healthy reproduction in women, fights cancer, and prevents premature aging. It comes from animal sources such as milk, eggs, meat, and fatty fish, all of which may be high in fat and cholesterol. But it also comes from plants, in the form of beta-carotene and other carotenoids, which are converted into vitamin A in the body. Beta-carotene is found in brightly colored fruits and veggies, which do not contain fat and cholesterol.

Vitamin C (ascorbic acid) is a water-soluble vitamin and powerful antioxidant. It is vital in protecting connective tissue, bones, cartilage, and blood vessels, as well as in healing injuries and forming collagen. Found in all citrus, vitamin C is also abundant in leafy green vegetables, strawberries, melons, and bell peppers. It works best when paired with other antioxidants such as flavonoids, phytochemicals, and other vitamins. Although vitamin C is often taken as a supplement, getting it from whole foods is easy.

Vitamin E is a fat-soluble vitamin that prevents oxidative damage in cells, keeping cell walls from breaking down by protecting the essential fatty acids within those cell walls. Vitamin E is best known for protecting skin cells from ultraviolet radiation (UV rays); it also keeps stored vitamin A from deteriorating. Green leafy vegetables (such as chard, kale, spinach, and mustard greens), almonds, sunflower seeds, brussels sprouts, and broccoli are great sources of vitamin E. Deficiency in vitamin E is closely associated with gastrointestinal disorders such as irritable bowel syndrome, celiac disease, and liver disease, in which nutrients and vitamins are poorly absorbed in the digestive tract. If vitamin E is low, it's best to supplement it along with vitamin C, vitamin B3, selenium, and glutathione. Vitamin E functions optimally when paired with these other nutrients and each plays an important role in protecting the body. As always, it's best to consume these nutrients as part of a colorful whole food diet, but sometimes it's necessary to supplement them, particularly for those with gastrointestinal disorders where vitamin levels are lower than average.

Minerals

Like vitamins, minerals are needed in trace amounts in order for cellular reactions to occur in the body. Magnesium, potassium, manganese, copper, selenium, sulfur, and zinc all play roles as antioxidants.

Magnesium assists in making white blood cells, works with other minerals to strengthen bones and teeth, and helps to control and maintain proper nerve and muscle function. Rice, sesame, kelp, almonds, figs, and apples are excellent sources of magnesium.

Potassium is vital for brain function, regulating muscles and nerves, and maintaining proper electrolyte and pH balance in cells. It has been shown to lower the risk of high blood pressure and maintain normal heart beats. The mineral is also vital in the function of the adrenals and other endocrine glands. Many veggies and fruits including chard, mushrooms, spinach, brussels sprouts, squash, fennel, avocados, bananas, figs, and raisins, contain an abundance of potassium.

Manganese is an antioxidant that activates numerous enzymes and has roles in protein, carbohydrate, and fat metabolism. It is necessary for blood sugar regulation, nerve and brain maintenance, sex hormone production, skeletal development, and immune system health. Manganese can be found in spinach, kale, raspberries, pineapple, garlic, grapes, maple syrup, oats, and garbanzo beans.

Copper is the third most abundant trace mineral in the body. It helps to protect the cardiovascular, nervous, and skeletal systems. Copper acts as a powerful antioxidant by helping the body lower cholesterol levels and preventing atherosclerosis in the arteries. Copper plays a key role in the development and maintenance of healthy hair and skin, along with the production of melanin, which colors the skin, eyes, and hair. Copper is most abundant in crimini mushrooms, turnip greens, chard, kale, summer squash, sesame seeds, and cashews. Although clearly important, copper is one mineral that you do not want or need to consume more of through supplementation. The amounts found in foods are plenty.

Selenium acts as an antioxidant along with other vitamins and minerals to protect cells from oxidative damage. The mineral also enables the thyroid gland to produce hormones, fights cancer by boosting the immune system, and helps to lower the risk of joint inflammation. It's very important that food rich in selenium comes from organic and wild sources. Button mushrooms, broccoli, onions, grains, herbs, shrimp, cod, kelp, and eggs are the best sources of selenium.

Sulfur is vital for the formation of hair, nails, tissue, and cartilage. It is needed for metabolic activity and a healthy nervous system. Sulfur is used as an antioxidant to detoxify the body, boost the immune system and fight the effects of aging, as well as to fight age-related illnesses such as arthritis. There is no official Recommended Dietary Allowance or Dietary Reference Intake for this mineral, but as a guideline, you need more than 100 mg of sulfur per day. Sulfur can be found in dried beans, cabbage, eggs, fish, garlic, legumes, onions, poultry, and wheat germ.

Zinc is an essential mineral most often supplemented, although several whole foods are good sources of it. The mineral is involved in several aspects of cellular metabolism. It is required for enzyme activity, immune function, protein synthesis, wound healing, and DNA synthesis. Zinc also supports development and growth in the body. Oysters, crabs, beef wheat germ, pumpkin seeds, and legumes all contain zinc.

Text continues on page 44.

MAXIMIZE YOUR ANTIOXIDANTS

Super foods are foods with high concentrations of antioxidants, phytochemicals, vitamins, and minerals. Since
super foods are nutritious whole foods, they help us to
embrace our health, instead of thinking along the lines of
nutrient splitting or fighting disease. Implementing these
top super foods into your diet will allow you to reap all of
the benefits these yummy foods and herbs have to offer.
Here are the top 25 super foods:

1. Apples
Approximate ORAC Value: 3,224
(½ cup or 1 medium apple)

2. Avocado
Approximate ORAC Value: 1,933
(½ cup or 1 medium avocado)

3. Beans
Approximate ORAC Value: 8,093
(½ cup, mixed kidney, black,
pinto, dried)

4. Berries
Approximate ORAC Value: 5,090
(½ cup, mixed blue, black, rasp
& strawberries)

5. Broccoli
Approximate ORAC Value: 2,386
(½ cup, cooked)

6. Brussels sprouts
Approximate ORAC Value: 980
(½ cup, cooked)

7. Cinnamon
Approximate ORAC Value: 11,147
(1 teaspoon)

8. Cocoa
Approximate ORAC Value: 3,372
(1 teaspoon, unsweetened)

9. Coconut
Approximate ORAC Value:
Not available

10. Garlic
Approximate ORAC Value: 223
(1 teaspoon, approximately
1 clove)

11. Ginger

Approximate ORAC Value: 1,200
(1 teaspoon, ground), 618
(1 teaspoon, fresh)

12. Grapes

Approximate ORAC Value: 1,260
(½ cup, red), 1,118 (½ cup,
green or white)

13. Green tea

Approximate ORAC Value: 1,253
(½ cup or 4 ounces)

14. Kale

Approximate ORAC Value: 885
(½ cup, raw)

15. Kiwi

Approximate ORAC Value: 1,210
(½ cup or 1 gold kiwi),
882 (½ cup or 1 green kiwi)

16. Mushrooms

Approximate ORAC Value:
Not available

17. Oats

Approximate ORAC Value: 2,169
(½ cup, uncooked quick oats)

18. Oranges

Approximate ORAC Value: 1,819
(½ cup or 1 medium orange)

19. Pomegranate

Approximate ORAC Value: 2,341
(½ cup, juice)

20. Pumpkin

Approximate ORAC Value: 483
(½ cup)

21. Spinach

Approximate ORAC Value: 1,515
(½ cup, raw)

22. Sweet potatoes

Approximate ORAC Value: 2,115
(½ cup, baked with skin)

23. Tomatoes

Approximate ORAC Value: 546
(½ cup, plum tomatoes)

24. Turmeric

Approximate ORAC Value: 6,637
(1 teaspoon, dried)

25. Walnuts

Approximate ORAC Value:
13,541 (½ cup)

Herbs

Although typically thought of as flavor enhancers, herbs contain vital antioxidants. The most potent types of herbal antioxidants are flavonoids, compounds found in plants. The herbs with the most significant healing properties are garlic, green tea, bilberry, ginkgo, grape seed abstract, hawthorn berry, and milk thistle.

Garlic is probably the best-known herbal antioxidant, most notably for increasing heart health by helping to lower bad (LDL) cholesterol, regulate blood pressure, and inhibit blood clots from forming. It protects artery and capillary health, boosts immune system function, and has been shown to destroy cancer cells. Garlic is most potent when eaten crushed raw, but it is also available as a supplement in capsule form for people who can't stomach eating raw, crushed garlic cloves. We recommend eating, or supplementing, one to two cloves a day.

Green tea is among the most popular drinks in Asia for its powerful antioxidant properties. Super antioxidants specific to green tea are catechins, a group of polyphenols found in the bioflavonoid family. They have a long list of health benefits ranging from improving digestion to blocking cancer-triggering mechanisms. Green tea has been shown to prevent skin, lung, and stomach cancers, as well as lower blood pressure, boost immune system function, and stabilize blood sugar levels. For maximum benefits, consume a minimum of two to three cups of green tea a day.

Billberry fruit has been made into jams and pies for medicinal purposes for centuries. The pigment in the fruit has antioxidant properties that protect blood vessel walls and inhibit blood clotting. It has also been shown to stabilize blood sugar levels. Billberry can be found fresh in a health food store, dried in teas, or in capsules.

Ginkgo biloba has become popular for its ability to improve overall circulation, particularly in small blood vessels of the brain. Preliminary research on ginkgo has also been shown to improve memory and concentration, specifically related to Alzheimer's disease and other forms of dementia.

Grape seed extract, derived from the seeds of purple and red grapes, scavenges for free radicals in the brain, protecting against radiation, pesticides, and heavy metals. It has also been shown to improve conditions related to heart and blood vessels, such as atherosclerosis. Research also supports its use to mitigate eye damage, particularly macular degeneration and vision problems. Grape seed extract is typically taken as a supplement, in capsule or liquid form. It cannot be made by hand.

Hawthorn berry has a complex of flavonoids that promote a healthy circulatory system, decrease high blood pressure, treat angina, and improve congestive heart failure. Hawthorn is widely regarded as a safe and effective treatment for cardiac arrhythmia and early stages of heart disease. It is available in tea as well as capsule and liquid forms.

Milk thistle has been known for centuries as a liver detoxifier. The silymarin in milk thistle prevents liver toxicity because it acts as a potent antioxidant. Milk thistle has been shown to prevent cirrhosis, hepatitis, and jaundice of the liver, even in late stages of damage. It is available as a dried herb in capsule form, or as a liquid extract or tincture.

Many other herbs including basil and mint also provide antioxidant protection. Basil contains flavonoids, which help safeguard cell structure, and volatile oils, which have antibacterial properties. Mint helps soothe the digestive tract and ease stomach pains, and it has antifungal properties.

Integrating antioxidant-rich foods into our diet is just as important as understanding what those antioxidants do for us. Many antioxidants overlap in the foods we eat, and all fruits and veggies boast different nutritional value, making variety key. The ORAC scale is an easy-to-use resource for finding foods packed with powerhouse antioxidants. Just remember to actually eat these foods and not just read about them.

The best place to buy antioxidant-rich foods is a local farmer's market, to ensure freshness. Produce at farmer's markets is always in season, which is the very best time to buy it. If there isn't a farmer's market around, look for stores or supermarkets that carry a variety of fresh, whole, organic produce.

When integrating antioxidant-rich foods into meals, a good goal is to make fruits and veggies the stars of your meal, meaning there should be more of them than anything else on the plate. Find ways to incorporate fresh produce into every meal, even breakfast. We encourage our patients to make one night a week vegetarian night, with a main course of hearty vegetables and whole grains. Aim for 7 to 10 servings a day of fruits and veggies, or 2 to 3 servings per meal. See the Recipes, starting on page 74, for ideas on how to get essential nutrients into your body.

THE POWER OF GLUTATHIONE

Eating delicious, nutritious whole foods is the best way to get all the health benefits from antioxidants. But what happens if a person consumes lots of whole foods and the antioxidants can't work their magic in the body because of a biochemical mishap? You might be surprised to learn that there is an often-ignored necessity basic to proper antioxidant function: glutathione. Made naturally in the liver, glutathione is the most important antioxidant because it's found in every cell. It removes toxins from cells and protects against radiation. The body's ability to produce glutathione diminishes with age, making it necessary to find ways to increase production.

It's important to enhance the body's ability to produce glutathione; taking supplemental glutathione doesn't do the trick. It just can't substitute for what the body produces because the digestive system breaks down the supplement and inhibits its distribution to cells, where it needs to be. Luckily, it's possible to keep up the body's supply of glutathione, even as we age, by providing the building blocks needed to produce it: cysteine, glutamic acid, and glycene. All meats are high in cysteine, but they are not always good options unless the meat is organic and grass fed. Excellent food choices for glutathione enhancement include watermelon, walnuts, avocados, asparagus, broccoli, tomatoes, most dark green leafy vegetables, wheat germ, oats, and healthy cheeses such as ricotta and cottage cheese.

CHAPTER 3

The ORAC Scale

As you start to understand the biological significance of antioxidants, you may want to figure out how to get the most bang for your buck—that is, figure out which foods contain the most powerful antioxidants and concentrate on them. That's human nature. However, it's important to consume a wide variety of whole foods to get the maximum nutrition. Just because blueberries are a great source of antioxidants doesn't mean that a diet of just blueberries is healthiest. Remember, the whole is greater than the sum of the parts. The power of antioxidants resides in the unique blend of phytonutrients in each food and how those foods work together to enhance the biochemical processes in the body.

It's not necessary to guess which foods are good choices. There is a scientific way of measuring

the antioxidant capacities of foods: the ORAC
(Oxygen Radical Absorbance Capacity) scale, which
was developed by the National Institute on Aging,
an arm of the National Institutes of Health (NIH).
The ORAC scale tells us which foods are richest in
antioxidant levels as examined in vitro (in a test tube
or culture dish) in a lab. Critics claim that the scale
lacks credibility because the research is done in a lab
and cannot necessarily be extrapolated to describe
how antioxidants function in the human body.
However, it's clear that antioxidants are important
in quelling free radicals, which play a role in aging
and disease. So since a ranking of antioxidants exists,
it makes sense to use this information in deciding
which foods to buy and the types of meals to prepare.

Many different foods have been assayed
using the ORAC method. (An assay is a procedure for
measuring the activity of a biochemical in an organic
sample.) The actual testing involves mixing free
radical generators with fluorescent molecules, which
damages them, resulting in a loss of fluorescence.
Antioxidants are able to protect the fluorescent
molecules from the oxidative degeneration caused
by the free radicals. The ability of antioxidants in

various foods to slow the fluorescence decay is then calculated by recording and measuring decay curves.

The U.S. Department of Agriculture has published lists of ORAC values for many fruits, vegetables, nuts, seeds, herbs, spices, and grains. When comparing values, be sure that the units you're comparing are similar. Some evaluations compare ORAC units per gram of dry weight, others evaluate ORAC units in wet weight, and still others look at ORAC units per serving. Within each of these categories, similar foods can appear to have higher or lower ORAC values. For example, although a grape and a raisin have equal antioxidant potential (after all, a raisin is just a dried grape), the grape is assigned a lower ORAC value per gram of wet weight because it contains more water. Likewise, the high water content of watermelon can make that fruit appear low on the ORAC scale.

This table lists ORAC values in the lab's unit of measure, micromoles of TE/100g. One hundred grams is equivalent to a weight of approximately 3.75 ounces, or just under ½ cup of dry or liquid measurement (4 oz = ½ cup). When assessing the values in this list, it's best to visualize a ½ cup serving.

Naturally a ½ cup serving is not feasible for all items
on the list; for example, herbs and spices may be high
in ORAC, but are utilized in much smaller quantities
than other foods. Once again, we're reminded that
care must be taken to consume a wide variety of
antioxidant-rich foods. It's not enough to simply
increase one high-ORAC food in your diet.

 Keep in mind that many of the foods listed
specify "raw," even though you wouldn't eat some
of them—such as russet potatoes, beets, or dried
peas—uncooked. It just means that the lab tested a
raw sample of that particular food, or a whole group
of veggies listed under the category heading "Raw."
How do you know what the ORAC value of that
food is when cooked? You don't if the same food
isn't listed again as cooked, but you can compare
the values of raw foods and assume that ones with
relatively high values raw will also have relatively
high values cooked. Some foods are listed more than
once, so you'll know that broccoli, for example, has a
much higher ORAC value when cooked than raw.

THE ORAC LIST

FRUITS

	ORAC VALUE
WHOLE	
Acai berry	102,700
Apple, with skin	3,082
Apple, peeled	2,573
Apple, dried	6,681
Apple, Fuji, with skin	2,589
Apple, Gala, with skin	2,828
Apple, Golden Delicious, with skin	2,670
Apple, Golden Delicious, peeled	2,210
Apple, Granny Smith, with skin	3,898
Apple, Red Delicious, with skin	4,275
Apple, Red Delicious, peeled	2,936
Applesauce, unsweetened, canned	1,965
Apricot	1,115
Apricot, dried	3,234
Banana	879
Blackberry	5,347
Blueberry	6,552

All measurements are ½ cup unless otherwise noted

	ORAC VALUE
Cantaloupe	315
Cherry, sweet	3,365
Chokeberry	16,062
Cranberry	9,584
Currant, European black	7,960
Currant, red	3,387
Date	3,895
Date, Medjool	2,387
Elderberry	14,697
Fig	3,383
Goji berry	25,300
Gooseberry	3,277
Grape, red	1,260
Grape, white or green	1,118
Grapefruit, pink or red	1,548
Guava, red flesh	1,990
Guava, white flesh	2,550
Honeydew	241
Kiwi, gold	1,210
Kiwi, green	882

	ORAC VALUE
Lime	82
Mango	1,002
Nectarine	750
Orange, Mandarin (tangerine)	1,620
Orange, navel	1,819
Peach	1,814
Peach, canned, in heavy syrup, drained	436
Peach, dried	4,222
Pear	2,941
Pear, dried	9,496
Pear, green, with skin	1,911
Pear, Red Anjou	1,746
Pineapple, extra-sweet varieties	884
Pineapple, traditional varieties	562
Plum	6,259
Plum, Black Diamond, with skin	7,581
Prune	6,552
Raisin, golden	4,188
Raisin, seedless	3,037
Raspberry	4,882

All measurements are ½ cup unless otherwise noted

	ORAC VALUE
Strawberry	3,577
Watermelon	142

JUICES

Apple juice, unsweetened	408
Blueberry juice	2,906
Cranberry juice	865
Cranberry juice, white	232
Cranberry–Concord grape juice	1,480
Grape juice, Concord	2,377
Grape juice, red	1,788
Grape juice, white	793
Grapefruit juice, white	1,238
Lime juice, freshly squeezed	823
Lemon juice, freshly squeezed	1,225
Maqui berry juice	40,000
Orange juice, freshly squeezed	726
Pear juice	704
Pineapple juice, unsweetened, canned	568
Pomegranate juice	2,341

	ORAC VALUE
Prune juice, canned	2,036
Strawberry juice	1,002
BABY FOOD	
Apple and blueberry	4,822
Applesauce	4,123
Banana	2,658
Peach	6,257
Pear juice	414

All measurements are ½ cup unless otherwise noted

VEGETABLES

ORAC VALUE

RAW

Alfalfa seeds, sprouted	1,510
Artichoke	6,552
Arugula (rocket)	1,904
Asparagus	2,150
Avocado	1,933
Beet	1,767
Beet greens	1,946
Bell pepper, green	923
Bell pepper, orange	984
Bell pepper, red	791
Bell pepper, yellow	965
Broccoli	1,362
Broccoli raab	3,083
Butternut squash	396
Cabbage, green	508
Cabbage, red	2,252
Carrot	666
Carrot, baby	436
Cauliflower	829

	ORAC VALUE
Celery	497
Corn, yellow	728
Cucumber, peeled	126
Cucumber, with skin	214
Eggplant	933
Fennel	307
Kale, raw, 1 cup	1,770
Leek	490
Lettuce, butterhead	1,423
Lettuce, green leaf	1,447
Lettuce, iceberg	438
Lettuce, red leaf	2,380
Lettuce, romaine	963
Onion, red	1,521
Onion, sweet	614
Onion, white	863
Potato, red, with skin	1,098
Potato, russet, with skin	1,322
Potato, white, with skin	1,058
Pumpkin	483

All measurements are ½ cup unless otherwise noted

	ORAC VALUE
Radish	1,736
Radish seeds, sprouted	2,184
Snap beans, green	759
Spinach	1,515
Sweet potato	902
Tomato	367
Tomato, plum	546
Zucchini squash, with skin	180

COOKED

Artichoke, boiled	9,416
Artichoke, microwaved	9,402
Artichoke hearts	7,900
Asparagus	1,644
Bell pepper, yellow, grilled	694
Broccoli	2,386
Broccoli raab	1,552
Cabbage, black	1,773
Cabbage, green	856
Cabbage, red	3,145

	ORAC VALUE
Cabbage, savoy	2,050
Carrot	317
Cauliflower	620
Eggplant	245
Sweet potato, peeled	766
Tomato	406
SAUTÉED	
Bell pepper, green	615
Bell pepper, red	847
Onion, yellow	1,220
BAKED	
Potato, red, with skin	1,326
Potato, russet, with skin	1,680
Potato, white, with skin	1,138
Sweet potato, with skin	2,115
CANNED	
Corn, yellow	413
Ketchup	578
Tomato juice	486

All measurements are ½ cup unless otherwise noted

	ORAC VALUE
Tomato sauce	694
Vegetable juice cocktail	548
FROZEN	
Broccoli	496
Corn, yellow	522
Peas, green	600
Spinach	1,687

THE ORAC LIST / VEGETABLES

GRAINS

	ORAC VALUE
Flax hull lignans	19,600
Mush, blue corn with ash (Navajo)	684
Popcorn, air-popped	1,743
Sorghum, black	21,900
Sorghum, high-tannin	45,400
Sorghum, red	14,000
Sorghum, white	2,200
Sumac	86,800
Tortilla chips, reduced fat with Olestra	1,704

BRAN

Rice bran, crude	24,287
Sorghum, bran, black	100,800
Sorghum, bran, high-tannin	240,000
Sorghum, bran, red	71,000
Sorghum, bran, white	6,400
Sumac, bran, raw	312,400

CEREAL

Corn flakes	2,359
Granola, low-fat, with raisins	2,294

All measurements are ½ cup unless otherwise noted

	ORAC VALUE
Oat bran	2,183
Oats, instant, plain, dry	2,308
Oats, old-fashioned, uncooked	1,708
Oats, quick, uncooked	2,169
Oatmeal, toasted	2,175
Oatmeal, toasted squares	2,143
Quaker Oat Life, plain	1,517
Shredded wheat	1,303

BREAD

Butternut whole grain	2,104
Mixed grain (includes whole grain, 7 grain)	1,421
Oatnut	1,318
Pumpernickel	1,963

HERBS & SPICES

	ORAC VALUE
Basil, dried	2,815
Basil, fresh	200
Black pepper, ground	1,151
Cardamom seed	115
Chili powder	985
Chives, fresh	87
Cinnamon, ground	11,147
Cloves, ground	13,102
Cocoa, powder, Dutch-processed	1,675
Cocoa, powder, unsweetened	3,372
Coriander (cilantro) leaves, raw	214
Cumin seed	3,200
Curry powder	2,021
Dill weed, fresh	183
Garlic, raw	223
Garlic powder	278
Ginger, ground	1,200
Ginger root, raw	618
Lemon balm, leaves, fresh	250
Maqui berry, concentrated powder	3,125

Measurement for all herbs and spices is 1 teaspoon

	ORAC VALUE
Marjoram, fresh	1,137
Mustard seed	1,219
Onion powder	239
Oregano, dried	8,339
Oregano, fresh	582
Paprika	747
Parsley, dried	3,098
Parsley, fresh	54
Peppermint, fresh	582
Poppy seed	20
Sage, fresh	1,334
Savory, fresh	394
Tarragon, fresh	648
Thyme, fresh	1,143
Turmeric, ground	6,637

SWEETS

	ORAC VALUE
Agave, cooked	2,938
Agave, dried	7,274
Agave, raw	1,247
Chocolate, baking, unsweetened	49,926
Chocolate, dark	20,823
Chocolate, milk	7,528
Chocolate, semisweet	18,053
Chocolate milk, reduced-fat	1,263
Chocolate syrup	6,330
Cocoa mix, powder	485

All measurements are ½ cup unless otherwise noted

OILS AND VINEGARS

	ORAC VALUE
Apple vinegar	564
Apple and honey vinegar	270
Honey vinegar	225
Olive oil, extra virgin	1,150
Olive oil, extra virgin, with basil	684
Olive oil, extra virgin, with garlic	557
Olive oil, extra virgin, with garlic and red hot peppers	219
Olive oil, extra virgin, with parsley	766
Peanut oil	106
Red wine vinegar	410

NUTS

	ORAC VALUE
Almond	4,454
Brazil nut, dried, unblanched	1,419
Cashew	1,948
Hazelnut or filbert	9,645
Macadamia, dry roasted	1,695
Pecan	17,940
Pine nut, dried	616
Pistachio	7,983
Walnut	13,541

All measurements are ½ cup unless otherwise noted

LEGUMES

LEGUMES	ORAC VALUE
Black bean, raw	8,040
Black turtle soup bean, raw	6,416
Chickpea (garbanzo bean), raw	847
Cowpea (blackeye, crowder, or Southern pea), raw	4,343
Green snap bean, canned	290
Kidney bean, red, raw	8,459
Lentil, raw	7,282
Lima bean, canned	243
Navy bean, raw	1,520
Pea, split	524
Pea, yellow	741
Peanut, raw	3,166
Peanut butter, smooth, with salt	3,432
Pink bean, raw	8,320
Pinto bean, raw	7,779
Soybean, raw	5,764
Soybean, sprouted, raw	962

ALCOHOL

	ORAC VALUE
Cabernet Sauvignon	5,034
Red table wine	3,873
Rosé table wine	1,005
White table wine	392

All measurements are ½ cup unless otherwise noted

OTHER BEVERAGES

	ORAC VALUE
Chilchen (Navajo red berry beverage)	740
Tea, brewed	1,128
Tea, green	1,253

CHAPTER 4

Recipes

Take a look at the ORAC list, starting on page 54, and build your meals around the foods included there. When you shop at a grocery store, demand better foods by choosing only the whole foods typically stocked along the outer aisles. Better yet, support your local community by heading to a farmer's market whenever possible. We've learned that people are inclined to purchase more fruits and vegetables when shopping at a farmer's market at least once a week than at a chain grocery store. We encourage purchasing organic foods whenever possible because local organic produce and grains are guaranteed to come from healthy soil, free of pesticides, metals, and pollutants found in processed foods.

These deliciously nutritious recipes were created by our patient and friend, Chef Anna V. Zulaica of Presto! Catering and Food Services in Oakland, California. Our collaboration with Chef Anna yielded recipes that are natural, healthy, and high in antioxidants. Eating healthy starts with whole foods and high-quality ingredients that do not sacrifice flavor, and that's why we urge you to buy organic whenever possible.

The recipes are arranged in meal categories, including snacks and desserts, and we've supplied the approximate ORAC value for each recipe. Don't forget to calculate the ORAC value per serving so you can be sure that you're getting the extra antioxidant punch you're looking for in every meal!

BREAKFAST

Green Smoothie

Approximate ORAC Value: 16,795
MAKES 2 SERVINGS (1 QUART)

> 5–10 ice cubes
>
> 2 tablespoons coconut oil
>
> 1 cup frozen mixed berries
>
> 1 banana, cut in half or thirds
>
> 1 peach, sliced
>
> ⅓ bunch chard
>
> 1 handful spinach
>
> Water

Add ice to the blender first, then coconut oil, berries, banana, peach, chard, and spinach. Add enough water to cover one-third of the blender contents. Blend until smooth. Contains 10 to 12 servings of fruits and veggies.

Papaya-Spinach Smoothie

Approximate ORAC Value: 2,015
MAKES 1–2 SERVINGS

> ½ cup spinach
>
> ½ cup cubed papaya
>
> 2 tablespoons flaxseeds
>
> ¼ cup water*
>
> 3 ice cubes

Blend the spinach in a blender, then add the remaining ingredients and blend until smooth. Try experimenting with other fruits on the ORAC scale such as apples, berries, or apricots.

* Tip: If water is too bland for you, try using low-fat yogurt with 1 tablespoon of water, or add almond or soy milk instead.

Notes

- Green smoothies are one of the best ways to get up to 10 servings of fruits and veggies per blenderful!

- Blending the greens together first helps to break down their fibrous nature, which makes for a smoother smoothie.

- Swap out different fruits and veggies. Just be sure to include lots of greens!

- Save money by buying what's in season and freezing it.

- Use avocados, coconut oil, or nut butter to add protein and healthy fat.

- Sweeten with coconut oil, honey, agave nectar, or very ripe fruit.

Super Toast

Approximate ORAC Value: 5,000
MAKES 1–2 SERVINGS

> 1 or 2 slices 100% whole wheat bread
>
> 2 tablespoons unsalted almond butter
>
> 1 medium banana
>
> Ground cinnamon

Toast the bread and spread with almond butter. Cut the banana in thin slices and arrange on the toast. Sprinkle cinnamon, to taste, on top of the banana. A healthy, nutritious, and filling breakfast!

Notes

- Pair Super Toast with freshly squeezed orange juice, or tea, for a complete anti-oxidant breakfast.

- Make sure your bread is 100% whole wheat.

- Cinnamon is a wonder spice high on the ORAC scale.

Berries Deluxe Oatmeal

Approximate ORAC Value: 9,000
MAKES 1–2 SERVINGS

½ cup old-fashioned oats

1 cup plain soy milk

½ teaspoon vanilla extract

½ cup mixed fresh blueberries, strawberries, and blackberries (halve or quarter bigger berries)

1 tablespoon toasted pecans

Cook the oats on the stovetop per the package directions, but add the soymilk and vanilla instead of water. Once cooked, mix in fresh berries and top with toasted pecans.

Notes

- Toasting nuts is quick and easy. Warm a flat pan over medium to high heat, add the pecans, and stir so they don't burn. Remove them from the pan as soon as you smell a buttery, toasty aroma.

- Add as many berries as you like; they pack a high antioxidant punch.

- Oats are an amazing super food, but you can substitute other whole grains such as barley, quinoa, or farro.

Frittata

Approximate ORAC Value: 5,000
MAKES 4–5 SERVINGS

> 1 small white onion, cut in half and sliced into thin half moons
>
> 3–4 tablespoons extra virgin olive oil, divided
>
> ¼ teaspoon brown sugar
>
> 1 large zucchini, cut in half lengthwise and sliced into half moons
>
> 1 garlic clove, minced

1 cup thinly sliced crimini mushrooms

1 large tablespoon chopped fresh parsley or
   1 teaspoon dried parsley

2–3 heaping tablespoons finely chopped
   fresh basil

2 cups spinach

4 whole eggs plus 5 egg whites

½ cup grated low-fat Monterey Jack cheese
   (or pepperjack for more flavor)

½ cup 1% or 2% milk

Salt and freshly ground pepper

Begin by caramelizing the onion. Put the
onion slices in a small saucepan with 1
tablespoon oil over medium heat, and add
sugar, salt, and pepper. Let the onion sweat,
moving it every few minutes until light brown
and no longer stiff.

Preheat oven to 350°F.

Warm the remaining oil in a saucepan
on medium heat. Add the zucchini, and then
the garlic after a minute or so. After a few
minutes, add the mushrooms, parsley, and
basil, and then salt and pepper (the mushrooms

will release water and will not brown if salt is added right away). Once the ingredients are sautéed, turn off the heat and add the spinach.

In a large bowl, place the eggs and egg whites, grated cheese, milk, salt, and pepper. Whisk together.

Coat a 9-inch circular cake pan with cooking spray, and add the sautéed ingredients and caramelized onions first. Then add the egg mixture.

Bake on middle rack for 20 to 25 minutes or until knife inserted in the middle of the frittata comes out clean. Eggs can overcook, so keep a watchful eye!

Notes

- You can make individual servings of this frittata in a muffin pan for a quick, on-the-go breakfast for yourself or your kids.

- Broccoli and artichokes can be substituted for mushrooms and zucchini to increase the antioxidant power.

- Add herbs like fresh sage and thyme to increase flavor and antioxidant levels.

- Feel free to use button or oyster mushrooms instead of crimini.

LUNCH

Grilled Chicken with Black Bean Salsa

Approximate ORAC Value: 6,400
MAKES 4 SERVINGS

2 cups canned black beans

1 large Granny Smith apple, chopped

½ small red onion, finely chopped

1 serrano chile, seeds removed,
    then finely chopped

2 tablespoons chopped fresh cilantro

Juice of 1 large lime

Juice of ½ orange

Salt and freshly ground black pepper

4 boneless, skinless chicken breasts

Rinse the beans in a colander under cold water.
To make the salsa, combine all ingredients
except the chicken in a large bowl.
Refrigerate and let sit for at least 1 hour to
let the flavors combine.

Season the chicken with salt and
pepper and place on a preheated grill (or if you

don't have a grill, then in a skillet or grill pan
with 2 tablespoons of extra virgin olive oil).
Cook about 4 to 5 minutes per side. Close the
cover on the grill so the chicken comes out
moist. The easiest way to check if the chicken
is done is to cut into the middle of one breast;
if you see pink, it's not done. Serve the chicken
and salsa with a green salad tossed with olive
oil and balsamic vinegar, or red wine vinegar if
you prefer a tarter taste.

Notes

- The best chicken is organic, because it has
  been grass fed, and skinless, because skin
  has a lot of unnecessary fat. Breasts are better
  than thighs or wings because the meat isn't
  as fatty.

- Serrano is a thin, long green chile that is
  spicier than jalapeño. If you can't find it, try a
  jalapeño instead.

- Add tomato and bell pepper to the salsa to
  increase the antioxidant power.

Spring Salad Tossed in Arugula Dressing

Approximate ORAC Value: 5,120
MAKES 4–6 SERVINGS

Salad:

5 cups spring mix

1 large Granny Smith apple, chopped

1 large red pear, chopped

¾ cup halved cherry tomatoes

¼ cup toasted pine nuts

½ cup crumbled blue cheese

Dressing:

⅓ cup toasted pine nuts

1 large garlic clove

2 handfuls of arugula

¼ cup balsamic vinegar

⅓ cup extra virgin olive oil

Salt and freshly ground black pepper

In a large bowl toss together all the salad ingredients. Combine the dressing ingredients in a food processor, adding more balsamic vinegar if you like a sweeter dressing. Instead of adding the oil to the processor bowl all at once, you can drizzle it in until you get a thick, creamy consistency, almost like a pesto. Add salt and pepper to taste and mix. Top the salad with the dressing, tossing well.

Notes

- Heat extracts natural oil from nuts, hence toasted nuts have more flavor than raw. Warm a large flat pan over medium to high heat, then add the pine nuts and stir frequently so they don't burn. Remove them from the pan as soon as you smell a buttery, toasty aroma.

- Buy a small wedge of blue cheese and crumble it yourself. If you don't want to get your hands sticky, cut the cheese into small cubes. Don't buy precrumbled blue cheese in a plastic container—human hands did not crumble it, a machine did!

- Serve this salad for dinner by adding more seasonal vegetables and topping it with grilled chicken and a small whole wheat tortilla.

Insalata di Farro (Farro Salad)

Approximate ORAC Value: 1,000
MAKES 6–8 SERVINGS

> 2 cups Italian semi-pearled farro
>
> 1 zucchini, cut in half lengthwise and then into ¼-inch slices
>
> Extra virgin olive oil
>
> Balsamic vinegar
>
> Dried basil, dried oregano, and dried parsley
>
> 8 ounces fresh mozzarella in brine, cut into small cubes
>
> 8-ounce jar roasted red peppers, chopped
>
> Extra virgin olive oil
>
> ⅛ teaspoon dried marjoram
>
> Juice of ½ lemon
>
> Salt and freshly ground black pepper

Boil the farro in salted water just as if you were boiling pasta (you do not have to measure the water). Boil until the farro is soft but has a slight bite. Strain in a colander and set aside.

Heat oven to 400°F. Lightly coat a cookie sheet with olive oil spray. Lay the zucchini slices on the sheet. Drizzle oil and vinegar on the slices, and then top with salt, pepper, and as much of the dried basil, oregano, and parsley as you like. Bake until the zucchini starts to wrinkle and is soft to the touch.

To assemble the salad, mix the mozzarella and vegetables into the farro. Add a little more oil, marjoram, and lemon, and then salt and pepper to taste. Toss well. Serve chilled or right away so the warm farro melts the cheese.

Notes

- Substitute or add roasted asparagus and/ or brussels sprouts to the recipe for more crunch and antioxidants.

- Check the farro label! Some types must be soaked overnight. Choose one that cooks in 20 minutes.

- Marjoram is a relative of oregano. If you can't find it, use dried oregano.

- Feel free to experiment with herbs and spices, because they have very high ORAC scores.

Healthy Italian Pasta Salad

Approximate ORAC Value: 980
MAKES 4 SERVINGS

> 4 cups whole wheat penne pasta
>
> ¼ cup toasted pine nuts
>
> 2 cups halved or quartered cherry tomatoes
>
> 1 cup fresh mozzarella in brine, cut into small cubes
>
> 1 bunch fresh basil, cut into thin strips
>
> 4 tablespoons extra virgin olive oil
>
> Salt and freshly ground black pepper

Put a large pot of water on the stove to boil. Add a large pinch of salt and a drizzle of oil. Once the water is boiling, add the pasta and boil until the pasta has a slight bite to it ("al dente"), about 8 to 10 minutes. Strain the pasta, but don't rinse it.

To toast the pine nuts, warm a large flat pan over medium to high heat. Add the nuts and stir frequently so they don't burn. As soon as you smell the buttery, toasty aroma, remove them from the pan.

Toss all the ingredients together in a large bowl. The warm pasta will slightly melt the mozzarella.

Notes

- For a low-carb option, use bright leafy greens such as spinach or arugula instead of pasta, add a drizzle of balsamic vinegar, and toss.

- Experiment with other vegetables and herbs. High-ORAC vegetables include artichokes, broccoli raab, spinach, and asparagus, and thyme is a high-ORAC herb.

Healthy Cobb Salad with Vinaigrette

Approximate ORAC Value: 8,360

MAKES 4–6 SERVINGS

Salad:

5 cups spinach

1 cup sliced mushrooms

½ cup shredded carrot

½ large cucumber, cubed

½ can kidney beans

1 large avocado, cubed

4 strips turkey bacon, baked or cooked
   without oil until crispy

⅓ cup blue cheese or feta cheese, crumbled

Vinaigrette:

¼ cup balsamic vinegar (sweet) or red wine
   vinegar (acidic)

½ teaspoon reduced-sugar marmalade (any
   fruit flavor)

½ teaspoon Dijon mustard

½ cup extra virgin olive oil

Salt and freshly ground pepper

Place the salad ingredients in a large bowl. In a small bowl, put the vinegar, marmalade, and mustard, and then slowly drizzle in the oil as you whisk the mixture. Constant whisking emulsifies the oil and vinegar, dispersing the droplets of one into the other and creating a thick dressing. Add salt and pepper to taste. Pour the dressing onto the salad and toss.

Notes

- Crimini and oyster mushrooms have good flavor, but button mushrooms are perfectly fine.

- An English cucumber is a better choice than a standard cucumber because its skin isn't as tough and it has no large seeds.

- Add apples and grapes to punch up the flavor and pack an even higher antioxidant punch.

- When making vinaigrette, use a ratio of 1 part vinegar to 2 parts oil. You can use more or less oil and vinegar than the recipes calls for—just maintain that ratio.

Caprese Salad

Approximate ORAC Value: 1,711
MAKES 4–6 SERVINGS

>   2 cups (or more) balsamic vinegar
>
>   1 pound buffalo mozzarella,
>   cut into ¼-inch slices
>
>   1 bunch basil
>
>   3 large beefsteak tomatoes,
>   cut into ½-inch slices
>
>   Extra virgin olive oil
>
>   Salt and freshly ground black pepper

In a large saucepan, add at least 2 cups of balsamic vinegar (any kind is fine). Place over low heat for at least 20 to 30 minutes, keeping an eye on the pan. You don't want it to come to a boil; you just want a slight simmer. When the vinegar has thickened—reduced by more than half and looks like a glaze—remove it from the heat. Another way to tell it's done is to dip in a metal spoon; the vinegar should coat the spoon like syrup. Let cool.

Arrange the mozzarella slices on a large platter and top each piece with a large basil

leaf and a tomato slice. Drizzle the balsamic
reduction in very thin lines across the plate (a
little goes a long way). Do the same with the
oil. Season with salt and pepper to taste.

Notes

- Combining tomatoes with olive oil amplifies
  the nutritional benefit.

- Instead of using beefsteaks, try heirloom
  tomatoes for varied flavors and colors.

DINNER

Grilled Chicken Breasts Marinated in Ginger-Apricot Sauce

Approximate ORAC Value: 641
MAKES 4 SERVINGS

4 boneless, skinless chicken breasts

1 heaping tablespoon reduced-sugar apricot marmalade

½ teaspoon sesame oil

½ tablespoon finely chopped fresh ginger or ¼ tablespoon ground ginger

1 tablespoon Dijon or brown mustard

4 tablespoons cider vinegar

¼ cup extra virgin olive oil

1 large garlic clove, chopped

Place the chicken in a large sealable plastic bag and add all other ingredients. When you seal the bag, squeeze out as much of the air as you can and work the mixture into the chicken with your fingers by moving the bag around. Refrigerate on the bottom shelf for at least 2 to 4 hours.

Place the chicken on a hot grill, or if you don't have a grill, use a skillet or grill pan, and cook about 4 to 5 minutes per side. Close the cover on the grill or pan so the chicken comes out moist. The easiest way to check if the chicken is done is to cut into the middle of one; if you see pink, it's not done.

Notes

- Wild salmon can be substituted for chicken.

- Round out the meal with a salad to be sure you eat enough veggies.

- Add brown rice or whole grains for more phytonutrients.

Grilled Eggplant and Zucchini

Approximate ORAC Value: 2,177
MAKES 4 SERVINGS

> 1 large eggplant, sliced into ¼-
>   or ½-inch rounds
>
> 2 green or yellow zucchini, cut in half
>   lengthwise and then into thick slices
>
> Salt and freshly ground pepper
>
> Dried parsley, dried basil, and dried oregano
>
> Balsamic vinegar
>
> Extra virgin olive oil

Top each eggplant slice with a sprinkle of salt
to pull out excess moisture. After 10 to 15
minutes, dry the slices with paper towels. Lay
the eggplant and zucchini slices on edged pans
or sheets. Sprinkle with salt, pepper, and as
much of the dried herbs as you want, and pat
them down into the slices. Drizzle with vinegar
and oil. The eggplant will absorb a lot of the
liquid, so don't be afraid to pour it on. Place
the vegetables on a preheated grill and cook
for 2 to 4 minutes on each side. Turn them

once. Keep in mind that they'll cook faster on a charcoal grill than on a gas grill or grill pan.

Mediterranean Bowl

Approximate ORAC Value: 4,475
MAKES 4 SERVINGS

> 1 cup uncooked quinoa
>   or whole wheat couscous
>
> 16-ounce can artichoke hearts, chopped
>
> ½ cup pitted kalamata olives,
>   halved or chopped
>
> 8-ounce jar roasted red peppers, chopped
>
> ½ cup low-fat feta cheese, crumbled
>
> 1 cup cherry tomatoes, halved
>
> ½ small red onion, finely diced
>
> 1 tablespoon finely chopped fresh oregano
>
> 1 tablespoon finely chopped fresh mint
>
> Pinch of chile flakes
>
> Juice of 1 lemon
>
> 4 tablespoons extra virgin olive oil
>
> Salt and freshly ground black pepper

Cook the quinoa or couscous as directed on the package. Place artichoke hearts, olives, peppers, cheese, tomatoes, onion, oregano, mint, and chile flakes in a large bowl, and drizzle with lemon juice and oil. Put in the refrigerator for about 15 to 20 minutes to let the flavors combine. Fold in the cooked quinoa or couscous.

Notes

- Serve as a side dish with salmon fillets or chicken, or add chopped cooked chicken or albacore tuna to the bowl for a healthy salad.

- Regular couscous is fine if you can't find whole wheat.

- You can substitute heirloom tomatoes for cherry tomatoes.

- Experiment with the amounts of red onion, oregano, mint, and chile flakes—all are high on the ORAC scale.

Grilled Veggie Pizza

Approximate ORAC Value: 545
MAKES 4 SERVINGS

2 medium portobello mushrooms, sliced

1 small red onion, sliced into thin rounds

1 small yellow zucchini, sliced into thin rounds

1 tablespoon extra virgin olive oil

Salt and freshly ground black pepper

1 whole wheat pizza dough

2 plum tomatoes, thinly sliced

½ cup shredded part-skim mozzarella

¼ cup finely chopped fresh basil leaves

Preheat a grill, grill pan, or skillet to medium heat. Brush the mushrooms, onion, and zucchini with oil, salt, and pepper. Cook covered for about 6 minutes, turning once, until tender and brown. Remove from the grill. Separate the onion rings.

Preheat oven to 400°F. Spray or rub oil on a cookie sheet. Stretch the pizza dough with your hands or use a rolling pin on a floured surface. You can make whatever shape you like—it does not have to look pretty. Place the raw dough on the sheet, drizzle oil, and bake until crispy.

Remove from the oven, quickly add the grilled veggies, tomatoes, and cheese, and place

back in the oven just until the cheese is melted.
Top with basil.

Notes

- If the pizza is too dry for your taste, add
  low-sodium marinara sauce. Be sure to
  buy marinara or spaghetti sauce and not
  pizza sauce.

- Substitute vegetables or add more. Be creative!

- If you find the pizza too thick, cut the dough
  in half and use just that amount.

- Add some grilled chicken for protein. Since
  you are not baking the pizza very long, place
  precooked chicken on the pizza along with
  the grilled veggies.

Anna's Black Beans

Approximate ORAC Value: 5,800
MAKES 6–8 SERVINGS

> 2–3 cups black beans (1 small bag)
>
> 6–12 cups water
>
> 1–2 bay leaves
>
> ¾ teaspoon ground cumin, or to taste

Large pinch of sea salt

½ small white onion, sliced

2–3 whole garlic cloves

1–2 dried Chile de Arbol (dried skinny, flaky
  chilies), optional

Soak the beans in water overnight to cut the
cooking time in half the next day. You will also
need less water when you boil them because
they won't absorb as much. To cook the beans,
place a large pot of water (for every cup of
beans, use 3 to 4 cups water) over high heat.
Add all the ingredients. The amount of cumin
depends on how strong you like it. Bring to a
boil, then reduce heat to low and cook for a
couple of hours. Keep checking on the beans,
and occasionally stir and taste to see if they're
salty enough.

Notes

- If you don't have black beans, use other
  beans such as kidney or pinto.

- Add dried chile flakes, which are high on the
  ORAC scale, for extra spice and flavor.

Spice-Rubbed Salmon

Approximate ORAC Value: 1,848
MAKES 4 SERVINGS

> 2 teaspoons chili powder
>
> 1 teaspoon ground cumin
>
> 1 teaspoon brown sugar
>
> Pinch of salt
>
> Freshly ground black pepper
>
> 2–3 tablespoons extra virgin olive oil
>
> 4 (5 ounce) wild salmon fillets
>
> Juice of ½ orange
>
> Orange wedges, for garnish

Mix chili powder, cumin, brown sugar, salt, and pepper in a small bowl. Rub the mixture with your hands on each salmon fillet.

Heat a large nonstick skillet with 1 to 2 tablespoons of the oil and cook two fillets at a time. If you put all of the fillets in the pan and overcrowd it, the temperature of the oil will drop and you won't get a nice crunchy texture on the outside of the salmon.

Turn the salmon once and squeeze orange juice over the fillets. The fish is ready when it becomes flaky and you can separate it with a fork. Garnish with orange wedges.

Notes

- Serve the salmon with brown rice and a salad or sautéed vegetables such as those in the next recipe.

- Experiment with other herbs and spices high on the ORAC scale such as turmeric, curry, and tarragon.

Sautéed Vegetables

Approximate ORAC Value: 3,155
MAKES 4 SERVINGS

2 tablespoons extra virgin olive oil

¼ white or red onion, chopped

1 large garlic clove, finely chopped

1 pound asparagus, cut into thirds
   (about 2 cups)

1 medium green zucchini, sliced into rounds
   or half moons

1 medium yellow zucchini, sliced into
rounds or half moons

1 tablespoon chopped fresh parsley

Juice of ½ lemon

Salt and freshly ground black pepper

Heat the oil in a large skillet over medium-high heat. Add the onion and garlic and cook until fragrant, about 1 minute. Toss in the asparagus. After a few minutes, add the zucchini, parsley, and lemon juice. Season with salt and pepper to taste.

Notes

- Cut the fats ends off asparagus—they're tough and dry.

- When sautéing or cooking vegetables, put in the firmer vegetables first because they take longer to cook. Zucchini will get mushy if you add it at the same time as asparagus.

- The choice of veggies is up to you, so have fun. Try adding a medley of colorful vegetables such as bell peppers, squash, and eggplant.

Turkey Meat Loaf

Approximate ORAC Value: 2,780
MAKES 6 SERVINGS

> 1 slice whole wheat bread, crust removed
> and torn into small pieces
>
> ¼ cup low-sodium chicken stock
>
> 1¼ pounds lean ground turkey
>
> 1 large egg
>
> ¼ cup finely chopped onion
>
> ¼ cup finely chopped bell pepper
>
> ¼ cup finely chopped fresh parsley
>
> 1 teaspoon horseradish
>
> 1 teaspoon Dijon mustard
>
> 1 teaspoon Worcestershire sauce
>
> ½ teaspoon salt
>
> ¼ teaspoon freshly ground black pepper
>
> 4–6 medium sweet potatoes
>
> 16-ounces light sour cream, plain yogurt, or
> Greek yogurt
>
> 2 tablespoons fresh chives

Preheat oven to 350°F. Place all ingredients
except sweet potatoes, sour cream, and chives

in a large bowl and mix together to incorporate evenly. Lightly coat a meat loaf or other deep baking pan with cooking spray or rub oil on with your hands. Place the meat mixture in the pan. Bake uncovered for about 1 hour.

After the meat loaf is in the oven, pierce the sweet potatoes with a fork and place on another lightly greased pan, and bake for about 1 hour, or until you can easily stick a knife or fork into the potato.

Once the meat loaf is cooked, let it cool about 10 minutes, run a butter knife along the edges to loosen it, and invert it onto a large dish. Halve or quarter the baked sweet potatoes and arrange around the loaf. Put a dollop of sour cream or yogurt on every other potato and sprinkle chives on top.

Notes

- Sweet potatoes are incredibly good for you— they're loaded with antioxidants.

- Mix a whole grain, such as oats, barley, or spelt, with the meat mixture as a filler to make the meal loaf even healthier.

Kale and Roasted Squash Sauté

Approximate ORAC Value: 1,954
MAKES 4 SERVINGS

> 1 small butternut squash
>
> 1 bunch kale
>
> 2–3 tablespoons extra virgin olive oil
>
> 1 large shallot, finely chopped
>
> 2 cloves garlic, finely chopped
>
> ½ cup toasted pine nuts
>
> ¼ cup Parmigiano Reggiano shavings
>
> Pinch of red chile pepper flakes
>
> Salt and freshly ground black pepper

Preheat oven to 400°F. Cut the squash in half and scoop out the seeds. Coat a cookie sheet with cooking spray and place the squash cut-side down (this will help steam the squash by holding in the heat). Roast in the oven until the squash is tender to the touch in the middle. Remove and let cool. Once it has cooled, cut long lines down the inside of the squash and scoop out the wedges with a large spoon. Cut the wedges into bite-size cubes.

Meanwhile, chop the thick stems and spines off the kale and discard. Cut the kale through the middle and then cut across the width. Wash and pat dry. Heat the oil in a large skillet. Add the kale. After 1 minute, add the shallot, garlic, red pepper flakes, salt, and pepper. Sauté for about 3 more minutes, and then add the cubes of squash and pine nuts to the pan to cook for another minute. Put mixture into a serving dish and top with cheese shavings.

Notes

- Toasting pine nuts brings out their flavor. Warm a large flat pan over medium to high heat, then add the pine nuts and stir frequently so they don't burn. As soon as you smell the buttery toasty aroma, remove the nuts from the pan.

- Rather than buy cheese already shaved, purchase a small block of Parmigiano Reggiano and shave it yourself with a potato peeler.

- Substitute other greens such as chard, dandelion greens, spinach, or beet greens for different flavors and textures.

- Either winter squash or summer squash can be used, so you can make this recipe all year long.

SNACKS

Delicious Bruschetta

Approximate ORAC Value: 15,825
MAKES 6–8 SERVINGS

> 5–6 large heirloom tomatoes (different
> colors), cut into small cubes
>
> 1 large garlic clove, finely minced
>
> ½ red onion, finely minced
>
> 1 large handful of fresh Italian basil,
> cut into very thin strips
>
> 8–10 fresh mint leaves, cut into very
> thin strips
>
> 1 cup extra virgin olive oil
>
> ¾ cup balsamic vinegar
>
> Salt and freshly ground black pepper
>
> 1 French or Italian baguette

Preheat oven to 400°F.

Place the tomato cubes in a colander to allow the liquid to drain. Combine the drained tomatoes, onion, garlic, basil, and mint in a large bowl with the oil and vinegar, and season with salt and pepper to taste. Let the mixture sit for at least 30 minutes so the flavors can blend.

Slice the baguette into ¼-inch rounds. Drizzle a bit of oil and a dash of salt on each. Arrange the rounds on a cookie sheet and bake until the tops are toasty, a bit hard, and light brown on the edges. Take them out of the oven and let them cool completely.

Serve a tablespoon or two of the veggie topping on each toasted baguette slice as an appetizer or healthy snack.

Notes

• You can easily make the tomato mixture ahead of time and store it in the refrigerator or freezer. It's a definite crowd pleaser at parties!

Sweet Carrot and Apple Salad

Approximate ORAC Value: 24,780

MAKES 2 SERVINGS

> 2 large Granny Smith apples, cut into thin matchstick strips
>
> 1½ cups shredded or grated carrot
>
> ½ cup low-fat plain yogurt
>
> Handful of raisins
>
> 1 teaspoon ground cinnamon
>
> ¼ teaspoon ginger powder
>
> ¼ teaspoon curry powder

Put the apple strips and shredded carrot in a large bowl. Add the yogurt, raisins, cinnamon, ginger, and curry, and mix well. Place in the refrigerator for at least 30 minutes to let the flavors blend.

Notes

• Serve this salad as a side dish or as a topping on whole wheat pancakes or waffles.

• Add granola for a heartier snack.

- Experiment with different types of apples—
  the ORAC scale lists several varieties. Leaving
  the skin on the apples ups the antioxidant
  count.

Tzatziki Sauce

Approximate ORAC Value: 8,760
MAKES 2 CUPS

> 2 garlic cloves, very finely chopped
>
> 2 Persian cucumbers or ½ English
>   cucumber, shredded or chopped into tiny
>   cubes or strips
>
> ¼ cup chopped fresh mint leaves
>
> 2 cups plain 2% or 1% Greek yogurt
>
> Juice of ½ lemon
>
> 1 tablespoon extra virgin olive oil
>
> Salt and freshly ground black pepper

Mix the garlic, cucumber, and mint in a large
bowl with the yogurt, lemon juice, and oil.
Season with salt and pepper to taste. Let sit for
about 30 minutes to 1 hour to let the yogurt
soak up the flavors. Serve as a dip with veggies
or whole wheat pita.

Notes

- Tzatziki sauce is extremely versatile: It's great as a base for thick sauces, as a substitute for mayonnaise in dips or sandwiches, and as a topping for fish or chicken.

- Greek yogurt is best for this recipe because it is less watery than regular yogurt.

- Persian and English cucumbers have seeds tender enough to eat and soft skin that doesn't need peeling. However, you can use standard cucumbers if you like. Not peeling the cucumbers increases the antioxidant count.

Yummy Turkey Rolls

Approximate ORAC Value: 1,500
MAKES 1–2 SERVINGS

> 2 romaine lettuce leaves
>
> 4 slices roasted turkey breast
>
> 2 tablespoons brown mustard
>
> 2 slices cheddar cheese

On one romaine leaf, place two slices of turkey, spread mustard on top of the turkey, and top with cheddar cheese. Do the same with the other romaine leaf. Roll into a lettuce wrap for a healthy protein-packed snack.

Notes

· You can use chicken, fish, hummus, or roasted vegetables instead of turkey breast.

· Make sure any meat you use is not processed. Stay away from smoked meats, which almost always have additives and preservatives.

· To increase the antioxidant power of this recipe, add more veggies, such as broccoli, spinach, or carrots to the roll.

Healthy Granola Bars

Approximate ORAC Value: 25,900
MAKES 2–4 SERVINGS

2 cups old-fashioned rolled oats

½ cup raw sunflower seeds

1 cup sliced almonds

½ cup wheat germ

½ cup honey

¼ cup packed dark brown sugar

2 tablespoons unsalted butter,
   plus extra for pan

2 teaspoons vanilla extract

½ teaspoon kosher salt

2 cups chopped dried fruit, any combination
   of apricots, cherries, or blueberries

Preheat oven to 350°F. Butter a 9- by 9-inch
glass baking dish and set aside. Spread the oats,
sunflower seeds, almonds, and wheat germ
onto a half sheet pan. Place in the oven and
toast for 15 minutes, stirring occasionally.

In the meantime, combine the honey,
brown sugar, butter, vanilla, and salt in a
medium saucepan and place over medium heat.
Cook until the brown sugar has completely
dissolved.

Once the oat mixture is done, remove
it from the oven and reduce heat to 300°F.
Immediately add the oat mixture to the
liquid mixture, add the dried fruit, and stir to
combine. Turn the mixture onto the prepared
baking dish and press down, distributing
it evenly in the dish. Bake for 25 minutes.
Remove and allow to cool completely. Cut into

squares and store in an airtight container for up to a week.

Notes

- Dried fruits are chock-full of antioxidants.

- Add other nuts such as walnuts, pecans, and cashews to make the bars more nutritionally dense.

DESSERTS

Berry Sundae

Approximate ORAC Value: 1,500
MAKES 4 SERVINGS

> 4 tablespoons toasted sliced almonds
>
> 1½ cups quartered fresh strawberries
>
> 1½ cups fresh blueberries
>
> 1½ cups fresh raspberries
>
> 1½ tablespoons balsamic vinegar
>
> Pinch of black pepper
>
> 1 teaspoon lemon zest
>
> 1 teaspoon orange zest
>
> ½ teaspoon vanilla extract
>
> 16-ounce container vanilla frozen yogurt

Heat a skillet over medium-high heat. Add the sliced almonds and toast for about 4 minutes or until they smell done. Remove from heat. Heat all of the remaining ingredients except for the frozen yogurt in a saucepan until the liquid begins to bubble. Turn down the heat and simmer for about 15 minutes until it turns into a thick sauce. Remove from heat. Serve warm or cooled over a scoop of frozen yogurt and top with toasted almonds.

Notes

- Substitute plain yogurt for frozen yogurt— it will lower the amount of sugar and still satisfy your sweet tooth.

- Add crushed pecans and walnuts (toasted or not) for more crunch and a super food boost.

- Adding kiwi, peaches, and mango will further boost the antioxidant power of this dessert.

Sweet Potato Delight

Approximate ORAC Value: 3,682
MAKES 1–2 SERVINGS

> 1 small or ½ large sweet potato
>
> ½ cup low-fat vanilla or plain yogurt
>
> Pinch of ground cinnamon
>
> 2 tablespoons sliced or slivered almonds

Preheat oven to 400°F. Perforate the sweet potato with a fork, and then wrap in aluminum foil and place on a cookie sheet. Roast for about

30 minutes or until the sweet potato is cooked through. Remove from the oven and discard aluminum foil. Place in a bowl and mash, then top with yogurt, cinnamon, and almonds. Eat with a spoon.

Notes

- This is a very healthy alternative to standard desserts—almonds, cinnamon, and sweet potatoes are all high in antioxidants.

- Adding cinnamon to any dessert, or your morning coffee, will give a huge anti-oxidant boost.

Healthy Cheesecake in Vanilla Wafer Almond Crust

Approximate ORAC Value: 1,585
MAKES 12 SERVINGS

Crust:

3½ ounces vanilla wafers

½ cup slivered almonds

½ tablespoon ground cinnamon

¼ cup flaxseeds

Extra virgin olive oil

Batter:

8-ounces ricotta

8-ounces plain Greek yogurt

1 tablespoon maple syrup

Zest of ½ lime

Zest of ½ lemon

Juice of ½ lemon

1 teaspoon vanilla extract

1 egg

¼ cup all-purpose flour

2 cups fresh blueberries, blackberries, and/
   or raspberries

Preheat oven to 350°F. Combine all crust
ingredients in a food processor until the
mixture looks like flour (if too chunky it
won't form a crust). Drizzle oil into the
mixture until it holds together. Coat a muffin
tin with cooking spray. Mold the cracker crust
inside the muffin cups with your fingers so that
the crumbs go all the way up the sides. Bake
until the crust darkens and you can smell it. Let
cool completely.

In a large bowl, whisk together all batter ingredients except egg, flour, and fruit until there are no lumps. In a separate bowl, beat the egg with a fork. Add to the cheese mixture. Add the flour, mixing with a spatula until it is incorporated.

Pour the batter into the cooled crusts and bake at 350°F until you shake the pan and the filling doesn't jiggle anymore. Let cool completely before removing the cheesecakes from muffin tin. If crumbs get stuck on the bottom, sprinkle them on the cheesecakes. Top with fresh berries.

Notes

- The ricotta and Greek yogurt add a healthy element to the cheesecake without sacrificing taste.

- Fresh berries provide a zesty antioxidant kick.

Vegan Banana Muffins

Approximate ORAC Value: 1,509

MAKES 10 SERVINGS

> 1 cup whole wheat flour
>
> ½ cup all-purpose flour
>
> 1 teaspoon baking soda
>
> 1 teaspoon baking powder
>
> ½ teaspoon salt
>
> 4 bananas, mashed
>
> ¾ cup packed brown sugar
>
> ¼ cup unsweetened applesauce
>
> 3 tablespoons extra virgin olive oil
>
> ½ cup chopped walnuts, optional

Preheat oven to 375°F. Line 10 muffin cups with muffin papers. In a large bowl, mix together whole wheat flour, all-purpose flour, baking soda, baking powder, and salt. In another large bowl, beat together banana, sugar, applesauce, and oil. Stir the banana mixture into the dry mixture, stir in the walnuts, if using, then pour into prepared muffin cups. Bake for 18 for 23 minutes or until a toothpick inserted into center of muffin comes out clean. Do not overbake.

Notes

- Add the optional walnuts for crunch and antioxidants.

REFERENCES

Blach, James F. *The Super Anti-Oxidants: Why They Will Change the Face of Healthcare in the 21st Century*. New York: McEvans and Co., 1998.

Glassman, Keri. *Keri Glassman: A Nutritious Life*. September, 2010. http://www.nutritiouslife.com/pdf/orac_points_portable_guide.pdf

Mateligan, George, et al. *The Worlds Healthiest Foods*. The George Mateljan Foundation. September, 20 2010. http://whfoods.org/genpage.php

ORAC Values. 2010. http://oracvalues.com

Pollan, Michael. *In Defense of Food: An Eater's Manifesto*. New York: Penguin Press, 2008.

Pratt, Steven G., and Kathy Matthews. *SuperFood Rx: Fourteen Foods That Will Change Your Life*. New York: HarperCollins, 2004.

OTHER ULYSSES PRESS BOOKS

101 Healthiest Foods: A Quick and Easy Guide to the Fruits, Vegetables, Carbs and Proteins That Can Save Your Life
Dr. Joanna McMillan Price and Judy Davie, $14.95
With its one- to five-star rankings and quick reference lists, this book is the ultimate tool for finding and enjoying the incredibly nutritious foods that allow one to live longer, be healthier, and feel happier every day.

The Easy GL Diet Handbook: Lose Weight with the Revolutionary Glycemic Load Program
Dr. Fedon Alexander Lindberg, $10.00
Using these more accurate and sensible GL scores, *The Easy GL Diet Handbook* offers a plan for healthy weight loss and reduced risk of diabetes that's easier to follow. It also includes numerous foods that the Atkins, South Beach, and GI diets wrongly consider "off-limits."

The GL Cookbook and Diet Plan: A Glycemic Load Weight-Loss Program with Over 150 Delicious Recipes
Nigel Denby, $12.95
Offers a vast selection of GL-scored recipes so dieters can choose dishes they love while following a proven program for permanent weight loss without hunger.

To order these books call 800-377-2542 or 510-601-8301, fax 510-601-8307, e-mail ulysses@ulyssespress.com, or write to Ulysses Press, P.O. Box 3440, Berkeley, CA 94703. All retail orders are shipped free of charge. California residents must include sales tax. Allow two to three weeks for delivery.

ABOUT THE AUTHORS

Dr. Mariza Snyder and Dr. Lauren Clum are impassioned and dedicated doctors of chiropractic. Together they run The Specific Chiropractic Center in Oakland, California, where they focus on helping people to realize their own healing capacity. Working with patients has served as the platform for this book, as the authors realized that keeping it simple yielded the best results. They both graduated from Life Chiropractic College West in Hayward, California, and began practicing together in 2009.

Dr. Mariza completed her undergraduate studies at Mills College with a double degree in biology and psychology. She lives in San Leandro, California, and enjoys working out, traveling, and reading anything she can get her hands on.

Dr. Lauren graduated from Sonoma State University. After finishing chiropractic college, she practiced in San Jose, Costa Rica, before returning to her native Bay Area. She now lives in San Leandro, California, with her husband, Paul. They enjoy exploring the Bay Area, cooking, and spending time with their niece and nephews.